Songs of a Modern Disciple

by

JOSEPHINE ESTHER ROSS

Some of the poems in this book first appeared in the *Meher Baba Journal,* Bangalore, India, and are reprinted by permission.

Times New Roman typeface, 11pt.

THIRD EDITION

All rights reserved, including the right of reproduction in whole or in part in any form, except for review purposes.

Copyright ©2020, family of Josephine Ross

ISBN 978-0-578-63602-3

SECOND EDITION

All rights reserved, including the right of reproduction in whole or in part in any form.

Copyright, ©1989, by Josephine Esther Ross

Published by Manifestation Inc.
P.O. Box 991, North Myrtle Beach, South Carolina 29597

To the
ONE
WHO IS IN ALL
FROM WHOM ALL CAME
IN WHOM ALL IS CONTAINED
TO WHOM ALL SHALL RETURN

INTRODUCTION

My first meeting with Josephine Esther Ross was at a beautiful retreat on the Croton River, near Harmon, N.Y., in the Month of May 1932.

I had gone there hoping to meet Shri Meher Baba, the spiritual Master from India. As it turned out, I did not get to meet him on that occasion as he had left for California a few days before my arrival. However, I was happy to discover that his wonderful love radiation still pervaded the retreat, and the few people who were there, who were mostly young people near my age, were very friendly.

Josephine and her Mother, Mary Antin, were the first ones to greet me and to offer me the hospitality of the retreat. They and the others there told me quite a bit about Meher Baba's recent visit there, his life and his Mission, all of which served to confirm my own feelings about Meher Baba's spiritual greatness.

Not only was Josephine greatly uplifted by Meher Baba's Divine Love, but in addition, the well spring of inspiration was opened up within her and she began writing beautiful poems of love and devotion to her Beloved. We have kept in touch all through the years, and I have marveled at the clear beauty of her poetry. I was happy to see the first edition of *"Songs of A Modern Disciple"*, and now I am delighted to see the second edition becoming available to the increasing numbers who may find their own feelings for the Beloved so well expressed in Josephine's poetry.

Darwin Shaw

SONGS OF A MODERN DISCIPLE
by
Josephine Esther Ross

Poems expressing the mystic beauty of pure faith, of spiritual aspiration and growth of awareness of universal truths, are offered in this deeply communicative collection of verse by Josephine Esther Ross.

A disciple of the Spiritual Master, Shri Meher Baba, of India, where some of her poems have appeared, Mrs. Ross expresses, freely and movingly, the tremendous experience of meeting such a Master, and of discerning, through his teachings, the truth that God may be known to the individual without need of intercession.

> You call me Pagan;
> I worship trees;
> And make my prayer to sun and moon and stars,
> And passionately I love the good brown earth.
> I lift my voice in praise of shining rivers,
> And sunny, wind-swept hilltops,
> And crimson clouds reflected in still water.
> You call me Pagan, for I worship not in churches,
> Nor bend the knee to God or holy image,
> But out of doors I make my prayer to Beauty.
> And yet I know all things are one,
> And God and Beauty are but different names
> For the same Essence. . . .

In lines rich in spiritual beauty, the poet expresses the relationship of disciple to Spiritual Master, and the fullness of joy that comes of the soul's awakening to the Oneness of all things.

In "Song of Life" and other poems the theme continues, as an undercurrent, in verse touching upon contemporary life such as "Homemaker" ("A woman's life/ Is peace, if she will keep it so"); protests against war ("When all man's reckless cruelties are done,/ There will be oak leaves, and an autumn sun"); and "To a Little Girl" ("She whose eyes saw only beauty,/ And whose heart knew only Light").

Photo of Meher Baba taken in Bombay 1932 @Meher Nazar Publications

Thy Beauty, Lord, is Like a Thousand Blossoms

Thy beauty, Lord, is like a thousand blossoms
That lift their fragrant petals to the night,
And all the myriad jewels of the stars
Are pale beside the radiance of Thy light.

Thy purity is like a crystal lake
Reflecting on its surface calm and still,
A crescent moon and all Thy true perfection
The lonely deserts of my heart doth fill.

Ah, let me kneel in rapture now before Thee
And gaze forever on Thy radiant face,
Eternally enchanted by Thy beauty
Uplifted and enlightened by Thy grace.

For in Thy presence there is joy forever
And from earthly fetters sweet release,
Ah, let me kneel in spirit now before Thee
And lightly touch Thy shining robe of peace.

ACKNOWLEDGMENTS

To my beloved Master, Sadguru Meher Baba, who inspired me.

To my Mother, Mary Antin, who encouraged me.

To my good friend, Elvie Wachenheim, who made the publication of this book possible.

And to Georgene Kerchner, and my daughters, Margarita, Elizabeth and Rosemary, who said: "Now is the time."

CONTENTS

	Page
Aspiration	13
Reunion	13
Realization—For Kim	14
The Lotus	15
Thoughts of My Beloved	16
Visitation	20
Garden of Delight	22
Disciple to Master	23
Tryst	24
Love Increasing	25
The Divine Playmate	26
The Lesson	28
Parting	29
For the Beloved's Birthday	30
On Receiving a Letter from Baba	30
I Came to My Beloved	31
He Whom I Love Forever	32
Let There Be Peace	33
Sharing	34
Eternal Question	35
Peace	36
Fire That Burns at the Heart of Things	37
The Voice of Silence—To Grace Mann	38
The Lord's Servant	39
Anthroposophy—For M.A.	39
The Glimpse	40
Have I Known Love?	41
I Listen for Thy Song	42
O Love All Other Loves Beyond	42
God's Playmate	43
Victory	44

	Page
Communion	44
Dearer Than My Life to Me	45
Be Still	46
A Candle in the Window	46
Baba Visits Cairo	47
Life Abundant	48
Awakening	49
Master and Disciple	50
I. They Also Serve	50
II. Come Unto Me	50
III. Solution	51
Song of a Votary	51
Morning Thoughts	52
Out of My Sorrow	52
United	53
Of the Earth	54
Rebirth	54
Quest	55
Parting—For the Family	56
On the Cross—For Vivian Griffith	56
The Golden Cord	57
Christmas Carol	58
Prayer	59
Reproach—For W.B.T.	60
I Will Keep Faith	61
Adoration—To Baba	62
Attainment	63
Jesus Wept	64
Treasures	65
The Master to His Disciples	66
Crucified	67
Songs	68
Verses Written While Meditating on a Photograph of Shri Baba	69
I. The Wilful Disciple	69
II. Master and Disciple	69
III. O Love	70
Forget Me Not	71

	Page
Unity	71
Will You Come, My Beloved?	72
Instrument	74
Attempt at Recollection	75

Song of Life and Other Poems

	Page
Song of Life—To C.K.R.	77
Meeting with a Fellow Disciple—For Kenneth Ross	78
Transmutation—For Kenneth Ross	79
Rest—For Kenneth Ross	79
Love Waits Eternal—To Agnes and William Gould	80
Homemaker	81
Three Protests Against War	82
March 1938	82
Blind	82
Enduring	83
August Moon (A Lullaby)	84
Release	84
Spring o' the Year (Dance)	85
May Day Song	86
Song for St. Patrick's Day	87
To Gautama Buddha	88
Assurance	88
Spring Fever	89
To a Little Girl—To Millie Fanderlik	90
While Man Disputes	91
What Men Live By—To Ruth Morgan	92
Fireflies	93
Snow	94
Summer Wind	94
Wisdom	95
The Clock	96
Night Vigil	96
Song	97
When All Is Still	98
Beauty the Awakener	98
Seen in Brooklyn Heights	99

	Page
Remembering	99
The Willow	100
Windy Day	101
Moon-Mountain	103
To Meet the Spring	104
To a Wood Sprite	104
Photography—To Bobbie Simon	106
NEW POEMS - SECOND EDITION	**107**
The Rose of Sharon	108
Sacrament	109
All That I Am	110
Worship	111
The Master	112
NEW POEMS - THIRD EDITION	**113**
A Christmas Gift to Baba	115
AVATAR	116
Unattainable	118
O Thin White Flame of Purity	119
Autumn Morning	120
To a Fellow Traveller on Life's Road	121
To Baba on His Passing	122
Baba	123
Love Song	124

SONGS
OF A
MODERN DISCIPLE

ASPIRATION

From out the depths of doubt and fear
I'll raise aloft my dream;
Against the sky, like minarets,
My thoughts will softly gleam.

In silence and in purity,
Like forests under snow,
I'll build a sanctuary
For the Soul I long to know.

That temple of my dreams shall stand
Where all the world may see,
The Beauty and the Power
Of the Soul I long to be.

REUNION

O Love, had I forgotten,
Until I saw Thee here,
Down through all the centuries,
Lonely year on year?

Had I forgot Thy voice, Thy smile,
And all Thy winning grace?
Had I no recollection
Of the beauty of Thy face?

But if 'twere so, why did I then
Come running at Thy call?
My heart had not forgotten Thee,
Who art my all in all!

REALIZATION
For Kim

Transcendent Beauty, ever calm and pure,
    That calls me onward, upward, thru the night,
Oh, purge my soul of weakness and of sin;
    Illuminate my darkness by Thy Light!
(Eternal Beauty, deep within my soul,
    Oh, cleanse me, heal my wounds and make me whole!)

Yea, I have seen Thee on the mountain-top
    At dawn, when thrushes fill the air with song,
And tender willows brood above the path
    Where, white and purple, dew-drenched violets throng.
(Ah Beauty, hidden deep within my heart,
    I cannot longer live from Thee apart!)

And it was Thee I glimpsed one moonlit night,
    When water splashed into a garden pool,
And silence seemed embodied in a hill
    That curved against the sky, moon-bright, snow-cool.
(Eternal Beauty, breath within my breath,
    To live without Thee were my spirit's death!)

How many times I sense Thy Presence near
    As on the pages of some book I find
A rare, pure thought, a phrase like music formed,
    Creation of a consecrated mind.
(Ah Beauty, Thou the very core of thought,
    With what a price Thy flaming truth is bought!)

Ah, Thou hast trailed Thy garment thru my years,
    And left a haunting fragrance on the air
That will not let me rest, that lures me on
    To climb yet higher up the golden stair.
(Is it Thy Voice I hear above the strife?
    Beauty, I know Thee now . . . Thou art my *Life!*)

No more shalt Thou escape, Elusive One;
  I'll hold Thee fast by every art I know.
Together we shall fly thru starlit space,
  And leave the groping earth-souls far below.
(What form is this that at my feet lies prone?
  I lift my wings . . . singing, I soar . . . alone!)

THE LOTUS

A thousand-petalled Lotus, He,
  And I a wand'ring honey-bee.
Straight to His heart I fly, and then
  Away into the world again.
(Ah! bittersweet that mystic kiss,
  From dark despair to highest bliss.)

A many-sided prism, He;
  Each side a different quality.
Yet all are One, and He above
  Transmutes them by His power of Love
Into a perfect, matchless whole;
  Immutable, eternal Soul.

The Master of all life is He,
  Complete in His Divinity.
And who approaches shall be given
  A taste of hell, a glimpse of heaven,
A cup of fire, a sword of pain . . .
  Disciple, wilt thou come again?

A flaming-petalled Lotus, He,
  And I a questing honey-bee.
But now again unto His heart
  I'll fly, nor ever more depart;
To rest upon that couch of Gold,
  And let the petals 'round me fold.

THOUGHTS OF MY BELOVED

I

I will dance to my Beloved,
Because He is beautiful!
I will rejoice mightily
Because of His beauty.

At the thought of Thee, Beloved,
My heart leaps within me;
And the joy of loving Thee
Is more than I can bear.

Beloved, why art Thou so beautiful
As to break my heart?

II

My Beloved went away
And left me alone.
Now the nights are filled with longing,
And the days burn with the thought of Him.

The memory of His beauty
Is like a sweet perfume;
And I never cease to wonder
At the sweetness of His Love.

Beloved, why hast Thou chosen
To bless me with Thy Love?

III

My Beloved came to me
Like a thrush's song at daybreak,
Like roses in a garden,
Like snow upon the mountains in a crimson sunset glow.

My Beloved is more beautiful than these;
And a silver star at evening,
And a silver crescent moon,
Cannot rival Him in loveliness and beauty.

IV

I stand on a balcony near gently swaying tree-tops,
And a golden summer moon floods the world with her light.
Crickets and katydids fill the night with their shrill cries;
And my heart is lonely.

Where is He Whom I love more than all earth's beauty?
I look for Him among the stars
And find Him not.

V

They say that my Beloved is far away;
Across the seas, in distant lands He wanders.
He has forgotten; He cares no longer;
He will never come again.

Thus speak the foolish ones;
But I know better.
Is not my Beloved held forever in my heart?
How, then, shall He leave me?
Do not my thoughts dwell constantly on Him?
Then how can He forget?

VI

My Beloved is like a wheel,
Perfect in symmetry.
His beauty, like a sphere,
Has no beginning and no end.

VII

When my Beloved went away
He took my spirit with Him,
Leaving only the empty shell of my body.

I am as one who has died,
And yet lingers near the earth
Yearning for a joy that is past.

Beloved, why art Thou so cruel
As to take away the Soul
And expect the body to live?

VIII

My Beloved fulfills all my desires;
He is the answer to all my prayers;
The Reality hidden in my dreams,
And the secret beauty in the depths of my heart.

Were it not for my Beloved
I would no longer care to live:
For what is life without Beauty,
And Beauty without Love?

The thought of my Beloved is like a sharp sword through my
    heart,
Or a stab of flame in the darkness.

IX

Who shall praise my Beloved save I who adore Him?
Who shall understand His mystery?
He is like a thundercloud, shot through by lightning flashes;
He is like the gentle summer rain.

He gives of His beauty like the rich brown earth
That nourishes her children from the fullness of her great
   abundant life.
He lives only to bestow with lavish hand
The treasures of His wisdom and His love.

Who can appreciate the Giver
Save he who has received?

X

My Beloved smiled at me,
And my heart trembled with rapture,
And mountains burst into song.

But when my Beloved wept,
The world was hushed with awe
At the sight of so much beauty.

XI

When my Beloved speaks,
His voice goes out to the far corners of the earth,
Wave upon wave of harmony filling the air with music,
Like the mighty, vibrant chords of an organ,

And the birds are still,
Listening—wondering—
Not daring to stir so much as a downy feather
Lest they miss a single note of that Song.

But when my Beloved is silent,
I kneel at His feet,
And He reveals to me
The beauty of Truth.

XII

Beloved, Thou hast given me too much!
My soul faints under the burden of Thy Love.
My heart is full to bursting with the joy of knowing Thee.

Oh, what shall I give to Thee, Beloved,
In return for the gift of Thyself?

VISITATION

I

There was a night
When long, cool breakers
Roaring,
Flung themselves with wild abandon
Against the shore;
And sucking back, to gather strength anew,
Rushed forward with a cry,
Relentlessly to hurl
The fury of their seething, foaming crests
Against unyielding rock.

And then you came . . .
Like the radiance of moonlight on still, untroubled waters,
And I forgot the turmoil of the sea,
Knowing only your quiet presence,
And the shining of your eyes.

II

There was a night
When the sea murmured,
Sighing with weariness of centuries of toil,
Ages upon ages of endeavour to wear away the rock;
Heaving to vast rhythms beneath a starlit sky.

And then you came . . .
Like an elemental fury of wind
Shattering the stillness of the night
In one mad, glorious moment.
Gone my dreams of peace beside the sea,
And I was bruised and shaken, tossed and torn,
Whirled into the centre of your tempestuous self.

III

There was a night
When the sea shone silver with phosphorus,
And a thin, new moon hung low above the water.
And as I watched a rising mist
Obliterated moon, and far horizon,
And creeping forward softly, chilled the air
With silver moisture,
Till I scarce could see the line where sea and shore had met.

And as I stood, the fog enveloped me,
Soft and clinging, as gentle as a lover,
Without a lover's passion.
And all the world was lost and merged in one.

But you came not. . . .
Only, from out the heart of mist and unseen ocean
The crying of a sea gull reached my ears,
Accentuating all my loneliness.
And then was utter stillness
Almost tangible;
The stillness as when death and life are one,
Balanced in one long moment of Eternity,
When God has ceased to breathe,
And rests unconscious.

Fog—and a sea gull's piercing cry . . .

Was that a night, when, coming,
You found me unprepared?

GARDEN OF DELIGHT
(A Song to the Beloved)

The strong wind blows across the snow, Beloved,
And the stars are cold in the winter sky.
    But O Beloved, in my heart
    I have prepared a garden of delight for Thee.
    There roses bloom and hidden in the grass
    Are violets and sweet anemones.
    There, from a scented wood, the thrush pours forth
    His liquid song of love. . . .

The sheep tuck in their tails between their legs,
And huddle together, heads down, facing the storm.
Over them the blizzard rages, and the snow
Drifts high beside my window. . . .

    But in my heart, Beloved,
    There is sunshine, and the song of birds,
    And a brook wanders lazily through the meadows,
    Where daisies and buttercups nod in the gentle breeze,
    And in a pool, under the weeping willow,
    A fish leaps up, his iridescent scales
    Flashing like rainbows.

    O Beloved, on the earth is winter,
    But in my heart perpetual summer reigns:
    For where Thou art is love, and life, and laughter,
    The perfume of roses, the fragrance of myriad blossoms,
    In the world of men, Beloved, there is war,
    But in my heart a garden of delight,
    For Thou art there,
    And where Thou art, Beauty adorns her temple,
    And Love guards well the gate.

DISCIPLE TO MASTER

Was it to learn a worldly lore
   That Thou didst send me out from Thee,
That all my thoughts might be enmeshed
   In useless triviality?

Was it to learn how weak I am,
   That when temptations I must face,
I can so easily forget,
   And can so often fall from grace?

Was I not ready then to soar
   Up to those realms where Thou dost dwell,
Not being yet prepared for Heaven,
   But only for an earthly Hell?

Yet ever Thou dost send a thought,
   And ever Thou dost call my soul,
Reminding me that I am part
   Of an eternal, shining Whole.

Reminding me that though I stray
   In thought and deed from Thee apart,
Still Thou art waiting patiently
   Within the temple of my heart.

Beloved, cast me not from Thee,
   For I would be Thy servant still,
And though I struggle to be free,
   Bend my spirit to Thy Will.

Lead me now from out the maze
   Of selfish thought and low desire,
Cast me in Thy flames of Love,
   Cleanse my spirit in Thy Fire.

Burn away all worldly dross,
    That, emerging from the past,
I may know that I am free
    To be wholly Thine at last.

TRYST

I

Beloved, will the peace of the night
Be shattered by Thy coming?
Nay, Thou wilt come like the sighing of wind
In the palm trees,
And the night will be filled with the perfume of roses.
And the pool in my garden will reflect Thy beauty.

Thou wilt stand in the shadow
By my door,
And softly call my name.
In the dark, scented room within,
I will hear Thee, and arise,
And I will raise the curtain, and lift the latch,
And open to Thee.
In the silence of the starlit night
I will take Thee in my arms;
Thus will be our union.

II

It is not the hot breath of passion
That Thou bringest, O Beloved,
But a cool wind from the snow-capped solitudes of the
    Himalayas.
It is not wine in Thy cup,
But pure, life-giving water from the deep wells
    of the Spirit

(As it is written, "Whoso drinketh of this water,
 shall never thirst again.")
Nor art Thou a lover who would possess my body,
But a friend who releases my soul from all fetters,
And sets her free.

III

Beloved, when the soft wind sings thru the palm fronds,
And the night is cool under the silent stars,
Come to my door, and stand in the shadow and knock. . . .
Ah, grant that I may not be sleeping when Thou comest,
And let not my ears be deaf to Thy Voice,
Lest Thou should'st turn away, and go out into the
 darkness,
Taking Thy Light with Thee.

LOVE INCREASING

Beloved, before I knew Thee,
My heart was like a quiet pool
Unruffled by the winds of passion.

But when I glimpsed Thy beauty,
And looked into Thine eyes,
It was as though a stone were dropped
Into the very center of that pool,
Starting a silver ripple, that grew and spread
In ever increasing circles, till it reached
The outer boundaries.

And there the waters of my love o'erflowed
And covered all the earth, to the farthest horizon,
And went beyond, into Eternity. . . .

Beloved, since that first meeting of my heart with Thine,
I have filled Universes with my love for Thee!

THE DIVINE PLAYMATE

Let us run along the shore, O Happy One,
While the surging ocean waves sound their music in our ears
And beat against our hearts in mighty rhythms.

Let us rest where the sand is brightest gold, warm and soft
And the sun burns down upon us like a fire.
Golden sand and deep blue water;
Golden sun and clear blue sky;
And one white sail on the blue of the far horizon. . . .

I will gather strands of sea-weed, such as mermaids wear,
To hang like garlands 'round Thy neck,
To twine about Thy hair.
Now art Thou the joyous God-of-the-Sea,
Carefree and happy, laughter in Thine eyes.

I will fetch for Thee bright sea-shells, wonderful and strange,
Delicately carved and fluted, many-hued;
And lay them at Thy feet for Thee to choose
One, cone-shaped,
And hold it to Thine ear
And listen . . .
What dost Thou hear?
The murmur of the ageless sea is whispering within
But to Thee it is the voice of Thy Beloved.

Now let me listen. I hear
The voices of a myriad souls sighing for Thy love,
Calling through the ages for Thee to set them free.
This is their prayer:
"We,
Dwellers in the sea,
Cry unto Thee, O Lord.
We who are bound,
Facing a thousand lives of upward toil and struggle,

Long to be free.
Lift us, O Lord,
Up through the waves,
Up through the countless forms that yet are before us,
Lift us to Thee!"

Ah, Happy One, while we are so carefree,
Millions of souls are burdened with toil;
Thousands of hearts are weeping for Thy Love;
Hundreds upon hundreds are calling on Thy Name.
And winds of heaven, and ocean waves, and clouds, and
   golden grains of sand,
Lift up their voices in one ardent supplication:
'We who are bound
Cry unto Thee, O Lord.
Facing a thousand lives of upward toil and struggle,
We long to be free.
Lift us, O Lord,
Up through the countless forms that yet are before us,
Lift us to Thee!"

Wilt Thou answer, O Beloved?
Wilt Thou leave our happy play,
To go forth, dispensing mercy to a suffering Universe?
Linger yet awhile, I pray.
Even God must rest from toil,
And find sweet consolation in a game of make-believe;
Forgetting for an hour the burden of the world,
As He listens to the shouts of little ones at play;
As He hearkens to the song of one who loves Him.

So rest, rest . . .
I will sing to Thee, Beloved;
I will dance for Thee, Beloved, with a smile upon my lips.
This one hour Thou art mine—
Oh, let not the world intrude!
I would never let Thee go;

I would run with Thee along the shore forever and forever
With the music of the mighty waves sounding in our ears,
And the sweet, salt wind blowing in our faces,
And our feet lightly spurning the golden sand . . .

Forever and forever, my hand tightly clasped in Thine,
My heart beating with the rhythm of Thine Own.

THE LESSON

O Love, Love,
Let me clasp my arms about Thee,
And hide my face in the soft clouds
Of Thy hair.

Or wilt Thou rest
Thy head upon my breast
For one brief moment;
That I may know that Thou hast need of me?

Or let us sit,
My hand in Thine,
Upon the dais by the empty hearth.
And let me turn and look
Upon Thy Face,
Wherein lies all the beauty of my dreams.
And all the loveliness I never knew
Till now.

Ah Love, Love,
Thou hast looked away,
And I too turn my eyes from so much beauty.
In silence we two sit,
Hand clasped in hand,
And suddenly I am aware

(Oh Lesson taught and learned in utter silence!)
That Thou art gone,
And I am all alone.

One moment Thou art here beside me,
And the next
I am alone!
What Truth is this?
That Thou and I are one,
There is no other.
There is only I—or Thou—what matter
The name we give it?

Master, Master,
Let there be only Thou,
And let me be no more;
For only beauty is eternal,
And Thou art Beauty.

PARTING

A star was caught in a pine bough,
    And a wind went softly by,
And there was no one present,
    Only you and I.

The night was silent, silent,
    And our lips were silent too;
Only my heart was speaking,
    Voicing its love for you.

Alas! my heart was weeping,
    As we lightly said goodby;
But my lips were smiling, smiling,
    And a star fell down the sky.

FOR THE BELOVED'S BIRTHDAY

Beloved, come to me in the dawning,
When the pale mist covers the face of the world,
And the robins carol unseen from the tree-tops,
And the dawn wind sighs thru the pines
As the breath of One Who awakens. . . .

Beloved, O Beloved, come to me in the evening,
When the thin moon holds the star flowers in her arms,
And the crickets chirp in the long grass by the garden path
And the cool wind whispers in the oak leaves
As the voice of One Who revealeth secrets. . . .

O my Beloved, come to me in the deep of night,
When silence covers the face of the earth.
When all is still, then may I hear Thy step . . .
And the night wind sings in my heart,
And it is Thy Word and Thy Song.

Beloved, Beloved, knock softly on the portal of my heart
And open, and enter therein, and dwell with me.
In the deep, in the silence of the night,
Make my heart Thy sanctuary, for Thou art Beauty!
Make my heart Thine altar, for Thou art Love!

ON RECEIVING A LETTER FROM BABA

I

You blow like a storm through the garden of my heart
Bending the flowers low to the ground.
You are like a tempest in the trees,
Bending their branches low, low. . . .

You blow like a storm through my heart,
Leaving devastation behind.

II

Beloved, Beloved!
My heart cries out to you,
Beloved, come!
Bend me, break me, destroy me utterly!
Shake and toss the flowers in my garden;
Scatter their petals, crush them to the ground!
Oh come, Beloved!
Come again and again!
I adore you when you hurt me most.

You are like a tempest in my heart,
Destroying everything, save my undying love for you.

I CAME TO MY BELOVED

I came to my Beloved
Garlanded with flame;
And now my heart is beating
To the rhythm of His Name.

I came to my Beloved
Through sorrow and through pain;
My body had been strengthened
By wind and sun and rain;

My spirit had been beaten
By the storms of life,
Bruised, and yet triumphant
Over sin and strife.

I came to my Beloved
Sheathed in golden flame;
My life is now attuned
To the music of His Name.

HE WHOM I LOVE FOREVER

Out of millions and millions of people,
There is One Whom I love the best;
Who in goodness, and wisdom, and beauty,
Towers above the rest.

One face, out of millions of faces;
One smile that responds to mine;
One heart that is filled with compassion,
And beating with Love Divine.

Though prison walls were about me,
And chains bound down my feet,
Yet would my heart go soaring
That Beautiful One to greet.

Though my soul were fettered and shackled
With darkest sin and pain,
Yet would my heart leap upward
To praise my Lord again.

He never can really leave me,
No matter where He may roam
For my thoughts shall go forth like beacons,
Guiding the Wanderer home.

Though thousands of miles are between us,
Yet are we never apart;
For He Whom I love forever
Is imprisoned here in my heart.

LET THERE BE PEACE

Let there be peace within the heart,
    And quiet in the mind,
That God's great Wisdom may descend
    Enlightening mankind.

We cannot hear the "still, small voice"
    That ever seeks to guide us,
We cannot sense the shining Ones
    Who ever stand beside us,

Because we are so occupied
    With outer, daily strife,
And have no leisure to enjoy
    God's proffered gift of Life:

The quiet thought, the loving heart,
    The silence of repose;
The healing of a kindly word,
    The fragrance of a rose;

The sky at dawn, the stars at night—
    These are but gentle things,
Yet knowing them we are aware
    Of passing angels' wings.

Let there be peace within the heart,
    And quiet in the mind,
That God Himself may now descend
    To heal and bless mankind.

SHARING

My Love belongs to all the world,
    And not alone to me.
O Love, wilt Thou not take my heart
    And fill it full of Thee?

My Love has duties everywhere—
    No matter where He goes
My thoughts will be as close to Him
    As perfume to a rose.

But Oh! what bitter sorrow
    Never my Love to see,
Whose life belongs to all the world
    And not alone to me.

Yea, some may see Him daily,
    And rest beneath His wing;
I can only long for Him,
    And these poor verses sing.

Some day, I know that He will come
    On wings of Light to me,
And we shall dwell united
    Throughout eternity.

Ah Love! what bliss, what anguish,
    That I belong to Thee,
Whose beauty shines for all the world,
    And not alone for me!

ETERNAL QUESTION

Life within me beats against the imprisoning walls of flesh,
Longing to be free, soaring high above the mountains,
Flying free against the wide blue sky.

Shake the bars, Life! batter down the walls!
Free thyself forever from this flesh that hinders thy True
 Being.
Rise, up, up, to the very gates of heaven;
Swoop and soar thru cosmic spaces, whistling past a million
 planets.
Down, down, down to where the ocean rolls.
Plunge into its mighty waters to the sandy floor below.
Converse with strange sea creatures, fathoms deep beneath
 the surface;
Greeny gold the world below.
Golden sand and green sea water,
Waving sea plants, green and slimy, tugging, pulling at their
 roots,
Tugging, longing to be free.

All the Universe is thine to play in, Life that beats within me,
Yet thou dost choose to prison thyself within this finite body.
Thou art limitless and infinite, all power is thine, all beauty,
Why shut thyself within these walls? And choosing thus to
 limit
Why long so to be free?
Why ache, and cry, and fling thyself against the walls thy
 wishes raised,
Against thy self-made prison?

PEACE

Joy cometh in the morning,
The ancient psalmist said;
But Peace comes hovering near me
When at night I lie in bed.

With Joy I greet the morning
And pass the whole long day;
But peace comes flooding through me
When at night I kneel to pray.

I could not bear the flame of Joy
That makes the day so bright
If it were not that God is kind
And sends His Peace at night.

"Nothing," said Emerson, "can bring you peace but yourself, Nothing can bring you peace but the triumph of principle."

My mind was filled with thoughts of self,
So bold, so strong, so charged with greed,
When Truth came knocking at the door
And sought to enter in.
Out of the corner of my eye
I saw Him standing there.
But I was all on self intent
And gave no heed.

I shut my eyes and stopped my ears,
And raised a fortress 'round my heart.
But everywhere I turned I knew
That Truth was waiting patiently
'Til I should let Him in.

"I have no time for Thee," I cried,
"There is no room within my soul.
Until I saw Thee, peace was mine,
And joy."

But I could not discourage Him.
He waited quietly for me,
And though I turned and tried to flee,
Yet was He always by my side
No matter where I sought to hide
From Him.

At last the conflict wearied me,
For Truth was mightier far than I,
And sadly then I turned to yield
And bid Him enter in.

But when I looked where Truth had been
Lo! He was gone, and all around
Shone Light and Joy, and in His place
Stood Peace.

FIRE THAT BURNS AT THE HEART OF THINGS

Fire that burns at the heart of things,
Hidden from mortal sight,
When shall our eyes be opened
That we may behold Thy Light?

Deep at the core of every soul,
Fire of Life Divine,
When shall we strip ourselves of self,
And be completely Thine?

Eternal, forever unchanging,
Beauty without a name,
When may our feeble, flickering light
Merge in Thy glorious flame?

THE VOICE OF SILENCE
To Grace Mann

She bends and sways before
The winds that blow;
Anemone, as cool and pure
As snow.

The sun burns down upon her,
And the heat,
And noise, and angry bustle
Of the street

Well nigh o'ercome this dainty,
Fragile flower,
Whose heart cries out for rest and peace
Each hour.

O little one, forget not,
In the strife,
That deep within thee
Dwells Eternal Life.

The world will tempt and lure thee
From the Goal,
But stronger than illusion
Is thy soul.

The Voice of Silence calls
Within thy breast,
Nor will be stilled until thy soul
Finds rest.

THE LORD'S SERVANT

Unknown and unseen,
   Active or still,
Grant me the boon
   Of performing Thy Will.

In hidden places,
   Or out in the crowd;
Silent, unheard,
   Or shouting aloud;

Thy Name on my lips,
   Thy Love in my heart;
In Thy Holy Work, Lord,
   Grant me a part!

ANTHROPOSOPHY
For M.A.

Go softly, softly with the mind,
If you the Highest Truth would find;
For all of beauty dwells within
Thy soul, nor can the mind begin
To climb the mystic mount at last.
Beware lest mind shall hold thee fast
Caught in illusion. Know that He,
The Lovely One Who dwells in thee,
Is only seen by those who find
Their Highest Self beyond the mind.

THE GLIMPSE

Once, when the moon rose over the sea,
I'm almost sure that you came to me.
Once, when the dawn rose over the hill,
And all the world was hushed and still,
In that mystical hour at break of day,
I'm almost sure that I heard you say:

"Beauty is truth, and truth is love;
This is the Law in heaven above,
This is the Law on earth below,
And all you will ever need to know."
And then, as swift as a bird in flight,
You vanished into the morning light.

But what to me are beauty and love,
Or all the laws in heaven above?
And what to me is the earth below?
Ah, Beautiful One, I only know,
That weary and sad I will ever be,
Until you reveal yourself to me.

And now I stand on the moonlit shore,
Hoping that you will come once more;
And I watch the dawn come over the hill,
When all the world is hushed and still;
And I know some time you will come to stay,
Never again to vanish away.

HAVE I KNOWN LOVE?

Have I known love and love's sweet pain?
Not till that night I first saw Thee
Did I dream what love could be.

Have I seen beauty on the earth?
Never before, on land or sea,
Until mine eyes had gazed on Thee.

Have I known joy in years gone by?
Not till Thou camest, bringing Light
That put all fear and grief to flight.

Have I known anything at all?
Oh, not until I heard Thy call
Was I aware what life might be!
Lifted up in ecstasy,
Beholding God in everything,
Causing my heart to leap and sing,
Filling my very soul with awe
To know at last Thy Word is Law!

Now I surrender all I know,
Now I forget what I have been,
That I in Thee, and Thou in me,
May dwell throughout Eternity.

I LISTEN FOR THY SONG

Can walls shut out Thy Beauty,
Or noise drown out Thy Song?
Nothing can take away those things
That to my soul belong!

Can grief or pain or sorrow
Sever my heart from Thine?
Nothing can take away Thy Love
That is forever mine!

I wait in stillness, hoping
That Thou wilt come to me;
That I may be enfolded
In Thy serenity.

Oh, hear my prayer, Beloved,
And do not tarry long;
I yearn to glimpse Thy Beauty,
I listen for Thy Song.

O LOVE ALL OTHER LOVES BEYOND

O Love all other loves beyond,
  O Love so tender, pure and sweet,
Thou Sun that lights my very soul,
  I lie prostrated at Thy feet.

In all Thy beauty dost Thou come
  Responding to my feeble prayer?
Oh let my fainting soul be strong,
  The rapture of Thy Love to bear.

In all Thy beauty Thou dost come,
   And bending o'er me like a flame,
Thy purifying Presence lifts
   The burden of my sin and shame.

O Love all other loves beyond,
   Thou art the One Whom I adore.
Beloved Lord, do what Thou wilt,
   My heart is Thine forever more!

GOD'S PLAYMATE

I think that I was born
To make Thee smile!
To laugh and play with Thee
A little while.

To work and suffer always
Were quite wrong:
I'll ease Thy heavy burden
With a song.

When, wearied of Thy toil,
Thou seekest rest,
I pray Thee, lay Thy head
Upon my breast.

I think that I was born
To make Thee gay;
For even God Himself
Must sometimes play!

VICTORY

Oh, what has come between us,
   Now that faith has fled?
How fragile was the beauty
   That now seems cold and dead!

The fire of love once filled me
   With fierce and blissful pain;
It cannot be the joy I found
   In Thee was all in vain.

Who dares to say that beauty,
   Once glimpsed, can be forgot?
Nay, love can conquer reason
   When it argues God is not.

And love can conquer time and space,
   Circumstance and fear,
Revealing to the lonely soul
   That God is always near.

COMMUNION

My Love is like the night,
Aglow with many a star;
He blesses me with Light,
And calls me from afar.

My Love is like the day,
Joyous, bright and clear;
Though He is far away,
His Spirit hovers near.

Most beautiful art Thou,
Beloved of my heart!
And Thou art with me now,
Although we dwell apart.

Ah, weary mile on mile
Between Thyself and me!
And yet, I see Thy smile,
And I commune with Thee.

DEARER THAN MY LIFE TO ME

Dearer than my life to me,
And yet so far away;
Master of the Universe,
Companion in my play.

Thou Who art beside me,
Whom yet I cannot see;
Lover, child, or playmate,
Thou art all things to me.

Now I feel Thee nearer,
Closer than my breath;
And Thy love uplifts me,
Transcending life and death.

Beloved, wilt Thou hear me
When I kneel to pray,
Thou Who art so intimate,
And yet so far away?

BE STILL

If life could move as slowly as yon clouds,
Serenely sure as onward they must go;
Not shrinking from the goal that lies ahead,
Nor questioning the things they may not know;

If human souls, like trees before the wind,
Would yield their pride, acknowledging God's Will,
Rebelling not, then would He enter in,
And bid the turmoil of desire be still.

A CANDLE IN THE WINDOW

A candle in the window,
Its light will ne'er grow dim,
For I have put it there
To show my love for Him.

A candle in my heart,
And steadier its flame,
As I, in troubled hours,
Meditate His Name.

Yea, Faith and Hope and Love,
Have lit this fire in me;
Nor will it ever falter:
It burns to honor Thee!

BABA VISITS CAIRO
December 1932

Utter silence holds the desert now;
The sun burns down upon a world of sand,
Where rise the Pyramids against the sky,
Tombs of the kings who ruled this ancient land.

How many years since they were laid to rest
Beneath these stones men come from far to see!
Well did they build their monuments, thereby
Hoping their names would not forgotten be.

What secrets could their mummy lips reveal!
What priceless treasures of an ancient lore!
How rich in wisdom might the world yet be,
Could they return and speak to men once more!

But now comes One to Whom all things are known;
More powerful than any king is He;
And silently He looks upon the tombs
Of those great rulers of antiquity.

O Pharaohs, sleep no more, awake, arise!
The King of Kings has come to Egypt land;
He walks beside the river that you loved,
And leaves His footprints in the burning sand.

Rejoice! O desert peoples, near and far;
This Pharaoh comes to rule from realms above,
And conquers, not with armies and the sword,
But by the power of Purity and Love.

LIFE ABUNDANT

Thou art the light within my heart,
The vital force within my soul;
O Master, lead me from the part,
To full perception of the Whole.

O Joy that will not let me go,
That shines through e'en the blackest hour;
O Mystery I may not know,
O Wisdom and eternal Power;

Now teach me, guide me, show the way
To conquer sorrow, sin, and strife;
That night may yield to endless day:
Thy gift of more abundant life.

AWAKENING

My Love came to me unaware,
While yet I was asleep;
And offered me a golden gift,
To cherish and to keep.

Oh, would that I had been awake
To thank Him as I ought,
And give Him something in return
For that great gift He brought.

I know not what this treasure is
He brought me in the night;
Nor can I pierce its mystery
Until the morning light.

And now I can no longer rest;
I watch with eager eyes
To see the first faint streak of light
Against the morning skies.

Perhaps, when dawn has come at last,
He'll pass again this way;
And oh! suppose He says to me:
"I have returned to stay!"

I'll run to open wide the door,
And bid Him dwell with me;
That I may serve and worship Him
Throughout eternity.

MASTER AND DISCIPLE

I
THEY ALSO SERVE

Let me send forth beauty
Out of my pain;
Though Thou dost crush me,
I'll rise again.

Lonely and sorrowful
Though I may be,
All will I bear
Most cheerfully,

If thus I may serve Thee;
If only each day
I may help one soul
On its upward way.

II
COME UNTO ME

What is thy sorrow?
Why dost thou grieve?
Lift up thy heart,
Only believe,

And I on Myself
Will take all thy pain;
Nor will thy prayers
Be offered in vain.

Ah, how I love thee!
Only believe,
How great is My sorrow
When thou dost grieve.

III
SOLUTION

Wouldst thou know
True Joy at last?
Then take My hand,
Hold fast.

Wouldst thou know
Eternal Peace;
From all thy pain
Release?

Then, in Love
And Purity,
Look within,
And there find Me.

SONG OF A VOTARY

I bring the flowers of my heart,
   And place them at Thy feet,
And worship Thee, Beloved Lord,
   Who art so pure and sweet.

I bring the first-fruits of my soul,
   And give them unto Thee,
And kneel to make this offering
   In deep humility.

One boon I crave, O Blessed One:
   To gaze upon Thy Face,
Renewed, uplifted, and transformed,
   By Thy most holy Grace.

MORNING THOUGHTS

As morning breaks
I kneel to pray,
And thank Thee
For this bright, new day.

I know each flower,
Bird and tree
Were fashioned
In eternity

By Thee alone,
And all are Thine;
The whole creation
Is divine.

And as for me, Lord,
Let me be
A living poem
In praise of Thee.

OUT OF MY SORROW

Soft blows the wind,
Bringing bird songs to me;
And I return
Thoughts of love to Thee.

Out of my sorrow
A new song I weave;
O my Beloved,
I pray Thee, believe,

All of my joy
And my hope is in Thee;
Nor do I care
What may happen to me.

UNITED

You call me Pagan;
I worship trees;
I make my prayer to sun and moon and stars,
And passionately I love the good brown earth.
I lift my voice in praise of shining rivers,
And sunny, wind-swept hilltops,
And crimson clouds reflected in still water.

You call me Pagan, for I worship not in churches,
Nor bend the knee to God or holy image,
But out of doors I make my prayer to Beauty.
And yet I know all things are one,
And God and Beauty are but different names
For the same Essence.
You prefer Christ, and I the earth's great beauty.
Yet did not One make both?
And is it not That One we both adore?
You in your church and I in sunny meadow,
You in a chapel, I on ocean's shore.
Then are we fellow worshippers, we two,
And Love shall guide us both forevermore.

OF THE EARTH

Of the earth, earthy,
Of the sky, pure,
Of the wind, clean and free,
Of the rock, steady, sure
Thus will I be.

Of the fire, Joy,
Of the sun, bright.
Of the rain, cool and fresh,
Of the moon, radiant, light,
Thus will I be.

Of the clouds, soft,
Of the stars, song,
Of the night, silence, peace,
Of the sea, mighty, strong,
Thus will I be.

REBIRTH

The mind strains at the body,
And the Spirit prods the mind:
The man leaps up: "I will follow the soul,
And leave all care behind!"

The Spirit herself is swifter
Than a comet in its flight;
Upward she soars to the farthest reach
Of the cosmic realms of Light.

The body lies panting far below,
The mind is all forlorn,
Till the Soul returns with power and joy,
And the man is newly born.

QUEST

I looked into each flower,
And listened to each bird;
I found Thee not, Beloved,
Thou wert unseen, unheard.

I wandered through the woodland,
Where trees grew straight and tall;
I saw Thee not, Beloved,
Nor could I hear Thy call.

I watched the clouds at sunrise,
And swallows flying low;
My heart was filled with longing,
For what? I did not know.

But now that I have found Thee,
Each flower, bird, and tree,
Reveals to me Thy Presence,
And only speaks of Thee.

PARTING
For the Family

Leaving the safe, familiar shores,
The vessel of my soul
Now ventures from the land of Part,
Upon the sea of Whole.

But Oh! the dear ones left behind,
With hands outstretched to me,
Who plead it is not wise to sail
Upon an unknown sea.

They think me cruel to leave them thus;
I wonder if they know
That if I looked back even once
I fear I could not go!

ON THE CROSS
For Vivian Griffith

Drop by crimson drop
The Lord's blood fell;
The agony He bore
What words can tell?

And now the whole world
Suffers on the Cross
Of pain, and hunger,
Doubt, despair, and loss.

Christ's Resurrection
They who mourned Him saw:
First suffering, then joy,
Is this the Law?

THE GOLDEN CORD

My eyes are blind, my ears are deaf,
And nothing do I know;
Into the abodes of Bliss
My spirit cannot go.

For I am chained and bound to earth,
Nor can I reach the height
Where my Beloved waits for me
Upon a throne of Light.

I cannot even touch His feet,
So far below am I;
And yet, I know that He can hear
My spirit's yearning cry.

For once my Lord looked down at me
From those far realms above,
And from His heart to mine He sent
A golden thread of Love.

And now I know that earthly bonds
Can never hold me fast,
For Love has spun a golden cord
To lift me up at last.

CHRISTMAS CAROL

May He Whose Mother laid Him
    Within a manger bare
Stretch forth His loving hands to bless
    And keep you in His care.

May He Whose star shone bravely
    To guide the Wise Men three
Ever guard your heart and soul
    Throughout eternity.

For in that stable lowly
    Was born our Heavenly King;
So let us lift our voices high,
    And with the Angels sing:

"Rejoice! rejoice! He cometh,
    A wise and comely Lord,
Who brings to earth salvation,
    Who speaks the healing Word.

"Rejoice! rejoice! He cometh,
    Our Brother, Master, Friend,
To rule in every loving heart
    His kingdom without end."

PRAYER

Let me be a flower
   In the garden of Thy Love,
Showing forth the wonder
   Of Thy Beauty from above.

Let me be a tree,
   Sheltering the world,
Bending to Thy Will
   With every leaf unfurled.

Let me be a stream
   In the desert of man's woe,
Carrying Thy Healing
   Wherever I may go.

Let me be a sheath
   For the world's blood-stained sword;
O let me be a servant
   In the kingdom of my Lord!

REPROACH
For W.B.T.

Your Real Self, the Spirit,
Is knocking at the door;
But you turn away and say:
"Come no more!"

Your Real Self, the Master,
Is standing at the gate;
But you turn your back and cry:
"Let Him wait!"

Your Real Self, the Soul,
You have crucified;
You could have saved Him
Had you only tried.

I WILL KEEP FAITH

I will keep faith with quiet things:
    With every feathered bird that sings,
With shining dew in fragrant flowers,
    With sun and rain and starlit hours.

I will remember morning skies,
    And rainbow wings of butterflies;
Cool mountain waters, crystal clear,
    And timid, lightly-treading deer.

I will draw strength from trees at noon,
    And from the radiance of the moon;
From forest glades where ferns may grow,
    And from the purity of snow.

I will keep faith with loving hearts,
    With those who practice kindly arts,
Who strive to comfort man's distress,
    Their hands outstretched to heal and bless.

With men of peace, where'er they be,
    I will keep faith eternally;
And with those Holy Ones Who trod
    This earth to point the way to God.

ADORATION
To Baba

Beauty hath woven for Him her fairest mantle,
  Love hath entwined in His hair sweet flowers of spring;
Light hath bowed at His feet in adoration,
  Filled with humility, angels have ceased to sing.

Clouds at dawn have blushed to crimson and rose,
  Because He hath passed and honored them with a glance;
Deep in the wood the flute of the hermit is stilled,
  And wondering nymphs have left their sylvan dance,

And drawing about them robes of shimmering green,
  Have stolen through forest glades where the ferns grow tall
To kneel at Love's feet and willingly there to surrender,
  Vowing henceforth and forever to follow Love's call.

Now through the depths of the forest a shadowy form
  Swiftly and silently glides, making never a sound;
Daintily treading over the springy mosses,
  Stepping lightly as one on holy ground;

And pausing a moment, startled, proudly lifts
  An antlered head, and, questioning, sniffs the air,
Gazing with wide-set, gentle eyes that are filled
  With a dawning wonder that Love could be so fair.

Hushed is the wind and trees have ceased to murmur;
  Even the voice of the brook is muted with awe;
And the rising sun hath paused on the threshold of heaven
  To worship the Master, Creator, and Giver of Law.

ATTAINMENT

Out of that which is imperfect shall rise that which is Perfect.
Out of man shall rise God.
Out of chaos shall come Beauty.
Out of darkness, Light.

And He Who is Perfect,
He Who is God manifest in human form,
He Who is all Beauty and all Light,
He Who has come forth from the Womb of Silence
Where the flames of the Eternal Fire blaze;
He—the Ancient One and the Ever Young;
The Creator and Destroyer;
The Splendid One in all the glory of His Majesty, and the
    tender Lover of men's souls;
He, and He alone shall lead mankind
From the path of destruction,
From the way of illusion,
Up, up the golden stairs that lead to the highest heaven,
Where there is Peace unending,
And silence that has deepened through a hundred thousand
    ages
Until it has become a Song of Bliss.

And He—the Perfect One—shall guide imperfect man
Through the realms of Light,
Up to the very throne of the Infinite Being,
And shall lift for him the veil that hides the Face of the
    Eternal.

Then shall man *see*, and seeing, understand.
Then shall chaos give birth to Beauty,
And darkness to Light;
And man shall stand at last,
Perfect in his Divinity.

JESUS WEPT

Twice have I seen tears in His eyes . . .

Like dewdrops glistening on jewel-weed blossoms are tears in
 the eyes of my Beloved.
As sweet and innocent as a very young child is He;
And as modest and gentle as a maiden, who dwells within the
 walls of her purity, all untouched by the clamoring world
 without.

His tears are as touching, and yet as passionless as those of
 a tiny baby, deprived of some trifling thing it wants—hurt
 for the moment—not comprehending—wondering. . . .
Ah! how cruel and heartless is he who can trample on a rose,
Or cause tears to glisten in the eyes of the Blessed One!

Would you willingly harm a helpless child that looks to you
 for protection and comfort?
Nay! you could not! Rather would you harm yourself.
Then watch every word and deed, lest you give sorrow, even
 for a moment, to Him Who comes to end sorrow;
Lest you cause the tears to shine in the eyes of One Who comes
 to dry the tears of all mankind;
Whose heart bleeds with every sorrowing heart;
Who weeps with every mourner, and bears the agony of every
 suffering soul.

Would you add an ounce, nay, the tiniest fraction of an ounce,
 to the pain which He already bears, so willingly, so pa-
 tiently, for you, and for countless millions of your brothers?
Would you cause God to weep?

* * *

Twice have I seen tears in His eyes,
And the world after a summer storm is not more beautiful,
 than tears in the eyes of my Beloved.

TREASURES

I haven't any silver,
   Nor have I any gold;
But in my heart a secret
   That never can be told.

I've neither land nor houses,
   Nor have I jewels rare;
But in my heart the image
   Of a Face surpassing fair.

Oh, I have neither wealth nor rank,
   Power, place nor fame;
But in my heart the music
   Of a well-beloved Name.

THE MASTER TO HIS DISCIPLES

In My heart is a jewel,
    A ruby of Light;
In My hand is a sword
    Of Power and Might.

Knowledge and Wisdom
    Illumine My mind;
All attributes holy
    In Me are combined.

Yet though I am strong,
    Majestic and wise,
It is Love you will see
    If you look in My eyes.

And though all the worlds
    Are upheld by My Grace,
It is Peace you will find
    If you gaze on My Face.

The whole of creation
    Is ruled by My Power;
Yet for you, in compassion,
    I labor each hour.

I am That which exists
    Without form, without name;
Eternal, unchanging,
    Forever the same.

CRUCIFIED

Beautiful One, where goest Thou,
With dancing feet and heart of love?

I go to bring the Living Light
To them that sit in darkness;
And to awaken Love Divine
In every weary soul.

Beautiful One, whence comest Thou,
With bleeding feet and heart of sorrow?

I come from them that sat in darkness.
Now are they rejoicing,
For I took upon Myself
The burden of their woe.

SONGS

Of what sing the birds,
   And what do they tell?
Of love in the woodland,
   A nest in the dell.

What sings the wind
   That goes wandering by?
Of life in the tree-tops,
   And clouds in the sky;

Of far distant lands
   Across the wide sea,
Where wanders my Lover,
   Still thinking of me.

Of what sings my heart
   Day after day?
Of the pain that it learned
   When He went away;

Of love that is strong,
   And joy that was brief;
Of hope that conquers
   All sorrow and grief.

But the song of my soul
   I can never repeat;
I placed it, a gift,
   At the Master's feet.

VERSES WRITTEN WHILE MEDITATING ON A PHOTOGRAPH OF *SHRI BABA*

I

THE WILFUL DISCIPLE

Not my will, but Thine, O Lord,
   And yet my will is strong,
And ere I listen to Thy Voice,
   Or hearken to Thy Song,

I have so many things to do,
   So many things to be;
Before I enter on the Path
   That leads at last to Thee.

So many wayward thoughts and deeds,
   Because my will is strong;
And yet, Thou wilt not let me go,
   Nor wilt Thou cease Thy Song.

A thousand wayward loves have I,
   Yet in my heart, I know,
There dwells Thy lovely Presence
   That will never let me go.

II

MASTER AND DISCIPLE

He draws a veil before His Face,
   He will not let me see
The beauty of His Countenance:
   His true Divinity.

He hides His Heart behind a cloud,
    His wisdom from my sight,
Lest I be overcome by Love,
    Or blinded by His Light.

But that pure Love He bears for me
    Will lift me up to see
Behind illusion's shrouding veils
    Eternal Verity.

And Oh! the love I bear for Him
    Will pierce the mystery,
And I shall lose myself at last
    In His Divinity.

III

O LOVE

O Love that fills my heart
    With only Thee,
O Love, O Fire,
    O Sacred Mystery!

If Thou wilt have me
    Suffer in Thy Flame,
Nor rest save in the
    Music of Thy Name;

Then take me, all
    Unworthy as I stand,
And let me only act
    At Thy command.

Be Thou my every breath,
    Be Thou in me
The motivating force
    That leads to Thee!

FORGET ME NOT

He passed this way, with brow serene,
   And from the skies above,
I heard sweet angel voices
   Proclaim the Lord of Love.

His eyes were shining like the stars,
   His hair was like the night,
He walked with calmness, and He wore
   A garment made of Light.

I knelt upon the earth, and saw
   That where the Lord did pass,
Little blue forget-me-nots
   Were hidden in the grass.

UNITY

   I pierce the many masks
      Which people wear,
   And see Divinity
      That's hidden there.

   I see not many
      But One Radiant Face;
   God's image doth
      The human one replace.

   I look into a thousand eyes
      And yet
   I only see the Soul
      Which men forget.

WILL YOU COME, MY BELOVED?

Will you come, my Beloved,
   In the peace of the night,
When the stars are throbbing,
   And the moon is bright?

Will you come, my Beloved,
   When the dawn is sweet?
Will you come, will you come,
   On dew-washed feet,

In a robe pure white,
   With a garland on your head;
Beloved, will you give me
   The Wine and the Bread?

Beloved, will you come
   In the dark of the night,
And offer me the Cup
   That is filled with Light?

Beloved, will you come
   With a flaming sword,
And speak to my soul
   The ineffable Word?

Beloved, do you see,
   I have flung wide the gate:
Beloved, O Beloved,
   How long must I wait?

* * *

Peace, O disciple,
   There is nothing to fear;
Lift up your heart and behold,
   I am here!

Wherever you go
  I am close at your side,
No place exists
  Where I do not abide.

Walls cannot hold Me;
  Chains cannot bind;
Whenever you seek Me
  With love, you shall find.

Time is My servant,
  And space at My Will
Is vanquished forever,
  Eternal and still,

Unmoved and unmoving,
  I dwell in your heart;
Disciple, be sure
  We are never apart.

* * *

Beloved, did you come
  In the peace of the night,
When the stars were throbbing,
  And the moon was bright?

Beloved, you are here!
  And the dawn is sweet.
You have come! You have come!
  Let me kneel at your feet,

And humbly receive
  The Wine and the Bread. . . .
O Beloved, there's a Light
  Shining all 'round your head!

INSTRUMENT

Let me be the perfume,
    As Thou art the flower,
Sending forth Thy Beauty
    Through the world each hour

Grant that I may be the song,
    As Thou art the bird,
Bringing peace and happiness
    Where'er its notes are heard.

And to pierce the heavy clouds
    Of the world's dark night,
Let me be the mystic ray,
    As Thou art the Light.

ATTEMPT AT RECOLLECTION

I sit by a quiet pool—slate-blue and shining, while golden leaves fall silently one by one to rest upon the water.

I am trying to remember—I go back along the centuries—back to the time when there was No Thing. I am trying to remember why I created Myself, for what purpose I made a Universe.

I wander over the earth, seeing, hearing, touching, smelling, and on all sides I find beauty.

Was it for beauty that I created thee, O gay, laughing brooklet, dancing over little, clean pebbles?

Was it for beauty that I made thee, O still pine wood, hushed beneath the absolute purity of drifted snow?

A wind sighs through the pines and I wonder: "Is that the breath of God—and am I God?"

Then have I done well in making thee, O wind, for here is peace; here in this quiet, winter wood I can be still and think My Infinite Thoughts. . . .

But I am disturbed—I cannot be at peace. Even here in this utter stillness I am aware of something that is inharmonious with the Whole. . . .

What is this hideous din of human cries, groans, shrieks, curses, prayers, that arises from the battlefields of history? Surely I did not make a thing so unlovely, so brutish. Did I create these gaping wounds? this agony of mortal pain? these thoughts of hate, and fear, and greed? How far have I forgotten My Original Purpose, if this is indeed the work of my hands! Had I foreseen this I think that I would rather have left the world unmade. . . .

And yet—not to have made a summer dawn? Not to have made a thrush?

But to millions of parts of Me dawn comes unloved, the thrush sings unheeded, while human bodies crowd into a subway, packed in, jammed against each other, breathing foul air, pushing one another aside, fighting for a seat, madly clutching a strap lest they fall and be trampled underfoot. Did I make this too? For what purpose? Or have I here forgotten Myself again? . . .

How could I forget a Plan that held within it the possibility of a Beethoven Symphony? What was my reason for creating Life that grew and changed through centuries of evolution till one form of it became a man, who, with the hands and brain I gave him, raised a slender shaft of stone and steel against the sunset sky?

Surely it was for Beauty that I built this towering city? Have I done well to make a bread line and a skyscraper? Which of these is according to the Plan?

I must think. I must remember. I have been dreaming through the ages while this seed of Life I planted has grown beyond all bounds, till it is out of control. Here is work for me to do. I must climb a lofty mountain and look out upon the Whole to gain a new perspective of the Universe. *I know there was a reason for it all.*

SONG OF LIFE
and
OTHER POEMS

SONG OF LIFE
To C.K.R.

Together down the steamy slopes of June
   While morning mists still hung above the river,
We ran—hand clasped in hand, and saw about us
   The meadow grasses sway beside the path,
And heard the high, sweet call of larks, and felt
   The burning heat of summer on our backs.

A honeymoon—a time of love and laughter,
   A time to live apart from all life's turmoil;
A time of sweet fulfillment and rejoicing
   Not caring what tomorrow's dawn must bring.

Together down the lush, green slopes of June
   We ran, carefree and singing as we went;
Nor saw the woods ahead, nor heard the rustle
   Of autumn's falling leaves as summer waned,
Nor saw the storm clouds darken the horizon,
   Before the chilling snows of winter fell.

* * *

Another spring, another June must ripen,
   But now I walk alone the path we trod,
Remembering all the youthful joy we shared,
   The love and laughter and the happy songs.

And now I hear the falling leaves of autumn,
   And now I know that life must lead to death,
And unafraid I feel the chill of winter,
   And watch the snow fall gently on your grave.

MEETING WITH A FELLOW DISCIPLE
For Kenneth Ross

Out of eternity
You come to me;
I look into your eyes
And there I see

Myself reflected!
Oh, in what dim past
Were we two parted,
Now to meet at last

Under these newer skies,
In this strange place?
What destiny now brings us
Face to face?

I clasp your hand
And cannot draw away. . . .
Must you depart so soon?
Could you but stay

What mysteries we
Might unravel! Here
We meet but for an hour,
And so dear

You are to me,
I cannot bear to part
With one who dwells so deeply
In my heart.

* * *

Out of eternity you come,
And then
Into eternity you go
Again.

TRANSMUTATION
For Kenneth Ross

Pure as the crescent moon upon the sky,
Silvery light against translucent blue:
Thus would I have the love you send to me,
And thus the love that I return to you.

Like downy seeds that ride upon the wind,
Filled with the promise of new life to be:
Thus shall my thoughts go speeding forth to you,
So shall your thoughts return again to me.

Oh, may this love that fills your heart, and mine,
Each for the other, lift us to that height,
Where we shall see our Master face to face,
And win at last our heritage of Light.

REST
For Kenneth Ross

Where has your soul been wandering so long,
That it has gathered star-dust on its wings;
That music, like a shadow, follows you,
So that my heart, responding, leaps and sings?

In what far corner of the universe,
Where fairies dwell, did they a garment bright
Fashion for you, so that you come to me
Robed in a mantle of the purest light?

O Wanderer, linger awhile, I pray,
For here beside you I find perfect rest;
My hand as safely held within your own
As though mine were a bird, and yours the nest.

LOVE WAITS ETERNAL

To
Agnes and William Gould

So many springs,
   So many birds returning,
So many summer noons,
   With hot sun burning.

Upon the good brown earth,
   The fields and flowers,
When only beauty marks
   The passing hours.

So many days
   When autumn's flaming glory
Repeats the lovely
   Ever-changing story

Of summer's end,
   And winter's silent cold,
When 'round the blazing hearth
   Strange tales are told.

But none so strange
   As that I wait for thee,
As I shall wait
   Through all eternity.

Ask me not why—
   The heart must have its reasons;
Love waits eternal
   Thru the changing seasons.

HOMEMAKER

A woman's life is little things:
   A baby's cry, a child's hurt knee;
The way the grasses grow along
   The path beneath the maple tree.

A woman's life is little things:
   The way the roses climb in June,
And how the grove is all transformed
   By silver fingers of the moon.

The long, straight line of red-tiled roof,
   The deep eaves where the shadows lie,
The smoke that from the morning fire
   Like incense rises to the sky.

The kettle singing on the stove,
   The timid rustling of a mouse;
The lamplight on a row of books,
   When evening quiet fills the house.

A seam to sew, a garment mend,
   A vase to fill with fern and flower;
The rush to gather in the clothes
   Before a sudden summer shower—

Day in, day out, of little things,
   She weaves a pattern to and fro,
To make a home: A woman's life
   Is peace, if she will keep it so.

For others crowds, and noise, and fame,
   Fantastic castles by the sea;
For her the guardian walls of home,
   The laughing babe upon her knee.

For others hustle, haste, and show,
   Poor tawdry baubles men can give
The foolish one who leaves her hearth,
   And has no time or place to live.

THREE PROTESTS AGAINST WAR

MARCH 1938

These things are good: The somber hills
Against the sky, the oak's bare bough,
And brown earth waiting for the plough.

Though armies march and tyrants shout,
As all the laws of love they flout,
Still stand the hills, serene and strong,
And spring awaits the bluebird's song.

BLIND

A fallow field beneath the sun,
   A lighted lamp when day is done,
A sturdy tree, a distant star,
   All simple things both near and far:

Unto all men such gifts as these;
   Unto all men the wind, the trees,
The quiet sky, the restless sea;
   Unto each soul . . . eternity!

And yet men quarrel and hate and fight,
   And shut their eyes against the sight
Of fertile fields beneath the sun,
   And lighted lamps when day is done.

ENDURING

Beauty of oak leaves in the autumn sun,
   Beauty of evening rest when work is done,
And lamps are lit, and quiet fills the night,
   And stars prick jewelled patterns made of light . . .

When tyrants' bombs destroy these homes we build,
   When all our loved ones have been maimed or killed,
When all these senseless cruelties are done,
   Remember oak leaves in the autumn sun.

O Man! remember beauty you have seen,
   Remember days when life was free and clean,
And build anew upon these patterns bright,
   A purer life, more near to heaven's light.

*   *   *

When all man's reckless cruelties are done,
There will be oak leaves, and an autumn sun.

AUGUST MOON
(A Lullaby)

August moon is hanging low,
    Hushaby, Lullaby.
All the world's a golden glow,
    Hushaby my baby.

Quiet night, with crickets singing,
    Hushaby, Lullaby.
Bats are flying, moths are winging,
    Hushaby my baby.

Flowers sweet perfume distilling,
    Hushaby, Lullaby.
Katydids' incessant shrilling,
    Hushaby my baby.

Sleeps the world beneath the moon,
    Hushaby, Lullaby.
Daylight cometh all too soon,
    Hushaby my baby.

RELEASE

I looked into the face of God,
    And it was wondrous fair;
For all the beauty of the world
    Was concentrated there.

I looked into the eyes of God,
    And they were wondrous bright;
And from them shone a tender love
    That filled my soul with light.

I looked into the heart of God,
   And there was wondrous peace;
At last my spirit found a home,
   And from its pain, release.

SPRING O' THE YEAR
(Dance)

Oh, come to the woodland, the robins are calling,
   The cowslip's in bloom where the brook runneth clear.
For winter is gone and a soft wind is blowing
   To tell woodland folk 'tis the spring o' the year.

The green buds are swelling, the brown earth sweet smelling,
   And green trail the willows where sup the wild deer,
And down in the glen all the wood folk make merry
   While Pan blows his pipe in the spring o' the year.

The farmer is plowing, his furrows upturning,
   And soon he'll be planting, for summer is near,
And down in the lane where the young folks go courting
   The hawthorne's in bud in the spring o' the year.

So come to the woodland, the robins are calling,
   The cowslip's in bloom where the brook runneth clear.
For winter is gone and a soft wind is blowing
   To tell woodland folk 'tis the spring o' the year.

MAY DAY SONG

My lover is ill and he's lying abed,
    But Oh! 'tis the first of May,
And what shall I send to my dearest love
    To gladden his heart this day?

I'll send him a violet plucked in the wood,
    With a stem so green and long;
I'll send him a bit of the blue, blue sky,
    And a note from a robin's song.

And here is a marigold yellow as sun,
    And there is a soft little cloud;
And I'll find an anemone fragile and white,
    And a columbine scarlet and proud.

The perfume and tang of the moist, brown earth,
    The freshness of sparkling dew,
And the green of the tender, new leaves I'll send,
    And the bluebird's joyous hue.

And Oh, for my lover who's lying abed
    I'll capture the essence of May,
And send it with sunshine and sweet spring winds
    To gladden his heart this day.

SONG FOR ST. PATRICK'S DAY

And a happy St. Patrick's Day to ye, my lads!
   Oh, may you be happy and jolly all day,
And may the Lord bless you and keep you in peace,
   And fill all your pockets with plenty of pay!

And a happy St. Patrick's Day to ye, my lads!
   Oh, I hope you are wearin' a bit o' the green,
For the fairest lads come from that land o'er the sea,
   And that's where the sweetest of lassies are seen!

And a happy St. Patrick's Day to ye, my lads!
   Now don't you be scrappin' and fightin' this day;
Just take it easy and don't work too hard,
   And all of your troubles will vanish away!

And a happy St. Patrick's Day to ye, my lads!
   The winter is gone and the spring's on the way,
And may the Lord guide you and keep you in peace,
   And give you His blessing by night and by day!

TO GAUTAMA BUDDHA

Buddha, calm and noble,
Sitting 'neath a tree,
Won't you come and play awhile
Joyously with me?

Why are you so quiet,
Silent and austere?
If I sang a song to you
I wonder, would you hear?

Buddha, full of Wisdom,
Always so serene;
Knowing things unknowable,
Seeing things unseen;

Heart of deep Compassion,
Eyes that are so kind;
If I sat beside you
I wonder, would you mind?

ASSURANCE

Lord, if the rose still blossoms,
   And the thrush still raises his song,
And the wind still sighs thru the pine trees,
   I know that nothing is wrong.

Lord, if the dew still sparkles
   On the meadow at break of dawn,
And the doe still stands in the forest,
   Guarding her new-born fawn;

And the bluebird wings thru the orchards,
    And the mourning dove still grieves,
And the maple is decked in autumn
    In her gold and scarlet leaves;

If the seed that's planted in springtime
    Still yields a harvest of grain,
Then, in spite of all man's folly,
    Life can be sweet again.

In spite of wars and tumult,
    The sorrows of man-made Hell,
Lord, if the rose still blossoms,
    I *know* that all is well.

SPRING FEVER

Curtains and rugs and furniture polish,
    Dishes and silver and linen so fair,
What do these matter when spring is calling,
    And lilacs are perfuming God's sweet air?

Crystal and glassware, vases and lamps,
    Scratches on woodwork and stains on the floor—
How can these hold me when spring in her glory
    Comes softly knocking at my back door?

Sheets and blankets that must be mended,
    Towels to wash and a stove to shine—
These petty trifles can never hold me—
    Beyond that door all Life is mine!

A house can be shelter, cosy and warm,
    But let it not hold us like prison bars;
Open the door for the wind to enter,
    Raise up the blinds and look at the stars!

TO A LITTLE GIRL

To
Millie Fanderlik

In her eyes were dreams of beauty;
　In her heart were dreams of love;
And the moonbeams shone in splendor
　All around her and above.

And her feet were dancing, dancing,
　As she went upon her way;
And her joyous laughter echoed
　Through each hour of the day.

And whoever gazed upon her
　Was enchanted by the sight:
She whose eyes saw only beauty,
　And whose heart knew only Light!

WHILE MAN DISPUTES

While man disputes,
   Sweet nature rules the day,
And scatters songs and flow'rs
   Along the way.

And still the roses bloom,
   The winds shall blow,
And mountains silent stand,
   Beneath their snow.

And still the sun will shine,
   God's life to bring;
And still at dawn and evening,
   Birds will sing.

What matter Democrat,
   Republican,
Or any other group
   Dividing man?

Beneath our hedge
   The violets grow in May,
And still shall grow
   When *we* have passed away.

WHAT MEN LIVE BY

To
Ruth Morgan

A little work, a little play,
   A little word of prayer;
The sky above, the earth beneath,
   Can Heaven be more fair?

A quiet hour when the sun
   Burns down upon the fields;
To one who watches silently,
   Earth all her beauty yields.

For God made hands to labor with,
   In simple tasks, and slow;
And feet were made that we might dance
   As to our work we go!

FIREFLIES

I

Stars in the sky,
And stars in the field.
The stars in the sky are steady,
Fixed in their places,
Immovable.
The stars in the field twinkle,
Here and there,
Everywhere.
A hundred of them, a thousand . . .
The field is alive with stars.

II

The little children of the stars
Are dancing in our field tonight,
While in the sky the grown-up stars
Shine with steady, grown-up light.

III

Perhaps the stars we see above
Are fireflies in some distant field;
And folk that live in those far lands
Look down at night,
Pointing thru a million miles
Of space to fireflies in our field,
And cry: "The stars are shining bright!"

SNOW

All about the house went Beauty,
    Gentle, pure and sweet.
Covering the ground with whiteness
    From her snowy feet.

Up and down the trees she ran,
    And with her snowy hand
Transformed the world of everyday
    Into a fairyland.

With loving care she went about
    All through the quiet night,
And softly laid upon the earth
    A robe of purest white.

SUMMER WIND

Do you hear God passing in the trees?
Softly, softly.
The leaves sway gently on their stems,
Bowing to Him.
They whisper among themselves. . . .
What are they saying?

WISDOM

To see the oak leaves, bronze and dry,
   Outlined against a clear blue sky;
To see the sun light up a pine
   Is to behold an art divine.
Why is it we are not enchanted?
   How can we take such things for granted?

To build a home upon the earth;
   To know the miracle of birth;
To feel the pulse of spring returning,
   Or watch an autumn bonfire burning;
Why do we seek elsewhere our heaven,
   When all these gifts are freely given?

The Book of God is all around us,
   The beauties of His world surround us.
To him who has the eyes to read,
   All Truth is found within a seed;
And in the form of bird or flower,
   There stands revealed the Eternal Power.

THE CLOCK

I love you! I love you!
   From morning till night,
And all through the hours
   When stars are so bright.

I love and adore you
   From night until morn,
And at that sweet hour
   When daylight is born.

From sunrise till evening
   I love and adore;
If days were but longer
   I'd love you still more!

NIGHT VIGIL

The clock, the little mouse, and I
   Kept vigil thru the night;
Each with his own tasks occupied
   Until the morning light.

I had my thoughts, the clock kept time,
   And mouse had things to do;
A nibble here, a scrabble there . . .
   The clock struck one, then two.

And on thru all the quiet hours
   Each went his secret way:
The clock, the little mouse, and I,
   Until the break of day!

SONG

Oh, life may be golden,
 Or life may be gray;
Clouded and gloomy,
 Or brilliant and gay;

But all through the pattern
 There runs like a thread,
The thought of the beautiful
 Things that you said!

Life may be busy,
 Or filled with delights;
Tiresome days,
 Or glamorous nights;

But all through the pattern
 There gleams like a star,
The thought of the beautiful
 Things that you are!

WHEN ALL IS STILL

The piping frogs are heralding the spring,
   And summer nights will hear the whip-poor-will,
And summer dawns the lark's sweet carolling;
   But Beauty only speaks when all is still.

Oft times around the house the strong winds cry,
   A mighty symphony of cosmic power;
Or gentle zephyrs thru the pine trees sigh,
   And bear the fragrance of some woodland flower.

But deep within the silence of the soul
   The Master comes, His promise to fulfill,
The outer voices merge into the Whole,
   And beauty speaks again when all is still.

BEAUTY THE AWAKENER

Let there be beauty all along the street,
   Laughter on lips and love in every glance,
And joyous sound of eager, running feet,
   And pulsing rhythm of the carefree dance;

Let gardens bloom and flowers their perfume blend,
   To make the world a sweet, enchanted place;
And trees before the zephyrs gently bend,
   A softly murmuring symphony of grace.

Let all earth's glowing loveliness combine
   To wake the seeds of beauty in man's soul,
That he may know his heritage divine:
   The wide horizons of the Cosmic Whole.

SEEN IN BROOKLYN HEIGHTS

O green willow, tenderly drooping between
    glowing, red brick walls,
Thy delicate grace transforms the uncompromising
    hardness of the brick
And makes of it a place in which to worship.

REMEMBERING

Deep in the chalice of sweet memory
I hold, like rare, old wine,
The thought of places I have known and loved:
A path between a meadow and a row of sturdy maples;
An old New England house beside a river;
An elm whose graceful branches curved and swooned
Above a dew-wet lawn. . . .

The Inn is quiet. I am left alone
Beside the whispering fire on the hearth.
Outside the waterfall sings thru the night,
Melodious, assured, and uncomplaining. . . .

And friends that I hold dear are with me now,
Upon this gracious, sun warmed, wide veranda . . .
Let my thoughts lightly rest upon each one,
Not grasping nor disturbing each free soul
Embodied in a form I know and love,
But brushing, as the wings of butterflies
Might touch a fern frond in a forest glade,
Their wings with mine; nor let me now infringe
Upon their solitude of suffering,
Lest I should mar the pattern God hath wrought.

THE WILLOW

The willow tree said to the cloud,
"Oh, I would be so very proud
If I were only free like you
To fly against the sky so blue!"

The cloud said to the willow tree:
"You have no need to envy me;
For I have sailed o'er land and sea,
And found no one as fair as you,
So delicate and graceful, too,
In lacy gown of palest green.
Of all the trees I've ever seen
You are most beautiful."

Just then the wind went wandering by,
Pushing the clouds across the sky.
He paused, and heard a weary sigh
Rising from earth—he turned to see
The cause of such despondency.

He saw the willow drooping low,
Her branches swaying to and fro.
He caught his breath in sheer delight
As he beheld that lovely sight.

Then low he bowed before the tree,
In reverence and humility;
And cried, "O Willow, pity me!
For I have roamed o'er land and sea,
And found no one as fair as you,
So delicate and graceful, too,
In lacy gown of palest green.
Of all the trees I've ever seen
You are most beautiful.

"I'd stay forever in this place,
Feasting my eyes upon your grace,
Delighting in your gown of lace
Outlined against the sky.
But winds may never cease to blow,
And ever onward I must go—
Onward over land and sea . . .
O lovely Willow, pity me!"

Then gently swayed the willow tree,
And murmured, "Sir, you flatter me!
But I will now contented be
To fill the place wherein I stand
With all the grace at my command.
And yet—I wish that I were free
To wander over land and sea;
Like yonder cloud against the blue,
Or even, gallant wind, like you!"

WINDY DAY

The wind comes dancing over the lea.
   Heigho! for a windy day.
The wind has a message for you and for me
As it comes a-whispering over the lea,
Swaying the grasses, rustling the leaves.
   Oh! 'tis a windy day.

Clouds go hurrying over the sky,
   Heigho! for a windy day.
Pines on the hillside moan and sigh
As winds-of-the-earth go whistling by,
Swaying the grasses, rustling the leaves.
   Oh! 'tis a windy day.

The wind is calling to you and to me
As it comes awhispering over the lea,
And thus calls the wind to you and to me:

"Oh, rise and go dancing over the lea;
Oh, rise and go swaying with grass and tree.
Hark, and I'll sing you the song of the sea;
Rise, and I'll teach you the dance of the lea.
Dance! and I'll give you the grace of a tree,
The beauty of clouds and the fragrance of flowers,
The silvery sweetness of cool April showers.
Dance! and I'll give you the wisdom of ages.
Dance! and be wiser than graybearded sages.
Dance with the leaves and with grasses bend low,
Dance 'til your body with joy is aglow!
Oh, sing with me, shout with me, laugh with me, love with me
Whirl with me, twirl with me, run with me, follow me!"
Thus calls the wind to you and to me:
"Lift up your voices and sing! sing! sing!"

* * *

The wind comes hurrying over the lea.
   Heigho! for a windy day.
The wind comes dancing over the lea
Singing the song of the surging sea,
And I call to the wind that goes whistling by:
"Oh, sing past the throne of the Lord on high;
Tell Him I thank Him for wind-in-the-sky;
Tell Him I'm happy and take Him my love
   And praise for a windy day!"

MOON-MOUNTAIN

I

Moon-mountain, powdered silver against a pale blue moonlit sky,
How black is the forest behind which you rise
In a serene curve of silent beauty!

II

I wander in the moon-drenched garden,
And a friend plucks for me two rose-colored blossoms,
And one pure white.
Dew-drops frost their delicate petals,
As a cool drink frosts a glass on a hot summer's day.
The great full moon shines strongly through the elm boughs,
Lighting the meadow.
I stand in the shadow of the pines,
And see bright pools of light on the soft lawn.
The air is cool and clear.
A cowbell sounds its note of gentle melancholy in the distance,
And close at hand water splashes into a little pond.

III

Now the mountain changes from silver to dark gray
And the moon swings higher in the heavens. . . .
Night moves on. . . .

TO MEET THE SPRING

Oh, I must away and over the hill
   To meet the spring, to greet the spring;
I must away and over the hill
   To welcome spring in the morning.

And first came a soft, caressing wind,
   And a rending of ice and a melting of snow,
And a piping of frogs from the marshes then
   And the sap was running in trees again.

Now from the roadside a song-sparrow calls,
   And my heart goes leaping and dancing to hear.
And out in the woods I will run, I will follow,
   For spring is arriving and I must be there.

I may find a violet, sun is so warm,
   And bluebirds are singing though orchards are bare;
And all through the earth is a pulsing and surging,
   A stir and a quiver of Life in the air.

So I must away and over the hill
   To meet the spring, to greet the spring;
For I heard when a robin was singing at dawn
   That spring will arrive in the morning!

TO A WOOD SPRITE

Come, Sprite!
Show me the dell
Where the bonny bluebell
In the wind doth sway.
Or the green wooded crest
Where the thrush hath her nest
And her eggs doth lay.

Show me the source of the swift-running brook,
And the well-hidden treasures of each little nook,
And to me declare
The secret of flower and fern and of tree,
Of butterfly, bird, and of wild honey-bee,
In the woods so fair.

Come, Sprite!
I would be wise
With the lore of the wild,
And dwell without fear;
Sharing his nuts
With the chattering squirrel,
His drink with the deer.

And when the owl
Doth call to his mate
And the stars shed their light,
On a soft fragrant couch
Of moss I would lie
And dream thru the night.

Fairies about me
Weaving their spells
To a magical tune,
While the wee furry folk
Go scampering past
In the light of the moon.

Ah, Sprite!
Friend to the wind
And the shining clouds
In a far-flung sky;
I'll follow thee,
Who art careless and free,
As the years go by.

PHOTOGRAPHY

To
Bobbie Simon

I

Out of the void his little face appears,
His perfect little body forward bent
As solemnly he contemplates his toes!

And now another: Ah, the precious imp!
A glint of mischief in those laughing eyes,
His mouth one wide, sweet smile.

Almost like being present at his birth
To see his image silently emerge,
As though a fairy waved a magic wand
And cried: "Come forth, thou hidden mystery!"

II

Out of the nothingness a star-bright flower,
A jewel on its pattern of broad leaves.
And here a butterfly—O fragile beauty!—
Is lightly poised upon a tree's rough bark.

III

Seeing these photographic forms emerge,
How can we doubt the great Creative Spirit,
Who, out of chaos, made a universe?

We, and the instruments we use, and these
Beloved forms we would perpetuate,
What are we but the photographic impress
Of God's Creative Thought upon the scroll
Of the eternal ether? We His Art,
As now we claim these pictures to be ours.

NEW POEMS
SECOND EDITION

The Rose of Sharon

Baba is a golden rose
   Glowing in the sky,
Shining like a golden sun
   Dazzling the eye.

Baba is a red, red rose
   A velvet passion flower,
Baba is the Rose of Sharon
   Filled with Love's sweet power.

Baba is a lovely rose
   Of deepest pink in hue,
Baba is the white, white rose
   Of Eternity.

Baba is a tired rose
   That droops in heat of sun,
Baba is a rose that died
   When His work was done.

Baba is the beauty of
   Roses everywhere.
Baba is the perfume of
   Roses on the air.

Baba is a golden rose
   In the heavens above,
Baba is the Sword of Power
   And the Rose of Love,

Sacrament

At the sound of Thy flute, oh Krishna,
My heart has missed a beat
And now I yield to Thy beauty
And kiss Thy lotus feet.

Life has no other purpose
Except to worship Thee.
Ah, what heavenly rapture
When Thou didst turn to me

And tenderly smiling proffer
A cup of sparkling wine,
A cooling draught of fire
That bound my soul to Thine, to Thine.

All That I Am

All that I have I give to Him,
    Each thing that comes and goes.
But, oh! How I grieve when each must go,
    He knows, He knows, He knows.

All that I want I give to Him,
    Desire upon desire.
Till at last they are all destroyed,
    In His sacred,. cleansing fire.

All whom I love I give to Him,
    For they are no longer mine.
And He will protect and cleanse them too,
    In the arms of Love Divine.

All that I am I give to Him,
    Of talents and gifts of art.
Till all are gone and I rest at last,
    Within His Sacred Heart.

Worship

Let me light a candle
   On the altar of my Lord.
And kneel and bow my head
   And contemplate His Word.

And as the incense rises
   And wreathes the candle flame,
Let me worship at the shrine
   Of His most Blessed Name.

And though I am unworthy
   To receive His Grace,
O, let me lift the veil that hides
   His most Blessed Face.

Lord, let me gaze in rapture
   Upon that which Thou art,
And feel the bliss of union
   With Thy most Sacred Heart.

And if Thou wilt accept me,
   My joy would be complete.
For I would yield my very self
   At Thy Most Blessed Feet.

The temple bells are chiming,
   High and sweet and clear
O heart, bow down in worship,
   My Lord, my Lord is here!

The Master

Like dawn upon the mountain
Or a sunset flame,
Like silver stars of evening time
The Lord of Beauty came.

Sweet clouds of incense hovered
Around Him and above.
He touched our lives with Glory,
He filled our hearts with love.

Mightier than the ocean,
Purer than the skies,
With tenderness and sorrow
Hidden in His eyes.

We bowed before the vision
Of God made manifest.
Our souls threw off their burden
And found in Him our rest.

And then the veil of splendour
Was parted and He smiled.
And Lo, we saw in wonder
He was but a child, a child.

NEW POEMS
THIRD EDITION

A CHRISTMAS GIFT TO BABA

Let me strew rose petals in Thy Path,
   And bring Thee the choicest fruits of the land,
And gems, and cloth of wondrous design,
   Fashioned by man's most skillful hand.

Let me lay at Thy Feet carpets of beauty,
   Rich in the colors of all earth's flowers;
And ruby-red wine in goblets of gold,
   And honors and titles and infinite powers.

Behold! Three Wise men brought gold and myrrh,
   And frankincense to burn at Thy shrine,
And humble shepherds brought lambs from their flocks,
   And offered their gifts to their Savior Divine.

But of all these gifts that I would proffer,
   And all that was brought by the Wise Men three,
I know there is naught Thou wouldst gladly receive
   Save only a heart full of love for Thee!

AVATAR
Sadguru Meher Baba

Above the tumult of the world,
   His Message, pure and sweet,
The Voice of Baba calls us
   To worship at his feet.

From Heart to heart His Love goes forth,
   From Soul to soul His Light,
From Mind to mind His Wisdom,
   From Life to life His Might.

His Beauty is a flaming sword,
   A beacon shining bright,
That penetrates the clouds of self,
   To guide us thru the night.

His wordless Word a challenge,
   His tenderness a flower,
That softens with compassion
   The impact of His Power.

Above the tumult of the world,
   His Message sweet and clear,
"Come unto Me, My children,
   Draw nigh, and have no fear.

"Come unto me, ye weary,
   As birds unto the nest;
Drop at my feet your burden,
   And find in Me your rest.

"Come unto Me, My loved ones,
   And find in Me release,
'Be still and know that I am God',
   The Messenger of Peace.

"'Be still and know that I am God',
   Be done with doubt and strife.
I am the Resurrection,
   I am Eternal Life.

"For I am He that cometh,
   And I am He that came,
The Crucified, the Glorified,
   Eternally the same.

"Behold! My pierce'd Hands and Feet,
   The thorns upon My Head,
And yet again I come to give
   The sacred Wine and Bread.

"And once again, upon the Path
   Which blesse'd Jesus trod,
I come to guide a sinful world
   Back to the Heart of God."

UNATTAINABLE

When I look into Thine eyes Belove'd,
  The sword of love pierces my very heart.
Thy Presence is like the fragrance of sweet flowers
  Dreaming beneath my window on a moonlit summer night;
And the touch of Thy hand is like a cooling stream
  In the parched desert of my life.

O my Belove'd!
  Why has the Creator Who fashioned the earth,
      and man and woman,
Lit the fires of passion in my soul
  Only to mock me with that which is unattainable?
Why must the Lord of Love and Light and Laughter,
  Show me perfection which I may
      only adore, but never possess?

The years of my life stretch before me, lonely and bleak,
  Filled with the sound of my weeping,
For I know that though I may prostrate myself before Thee,
  And offer my very life in adoration,
Still the peace of fulfillment will never be mine,
  And the bliss of perfect union will
      come to me only in my dreams.

O THIN WHITE FLAME OF PURITY
To Sadguru Meher Baba

O thin white flame of Purity that burns,
   Upon the altar of that mystic shrine
Within His Heart, I lift my heart to thee,
   That perfect beauty may be also mine.

O Self-Control that hewed those lines of strength,
   And power now reflected in His Face,
Let all Thy granite courage overflow
   From Him to me, my weakness to replace.

He knows, He knows, the coward that I am,
   He knows how weak I stumble through the night,
And only He can know the goal I seek,
   His Beauty, His Serenity, His Light.

AUTUMN MORNING

A flight of birds against the sky,
   Winging swiftly, free and high;
The morning sun above the trees,
   The oak leaves rustling in the breeze,

The golden corn, the tawny wheat,
   The dewy grass beneath my feet,
The infant pigs beside their mother,
   A kitten playing with his brother,

Is God not here where'ere I look?
   His Voice that murmurs in the brook,
The earth beneath, the sky above,
   Are but the outgrowth of His Love.

Is God not here within my heart?
   His Being manifested in each part?
His Life made flesh where humans dwell,
   A mystery too great to tell.

With mortal tongue, yet known to each,
   His gift of Heaven within our reach.
How can we doubt, how can we fear,
   While His Compassion hovers near?

The earth beneath, the sky above us,
   Are here to prove that He must love us,
And flocks of birds against the sky,
   Are but His angels passing by.

And sun, and moon, and stars so bright,
   All glorify the Lord of Light,
And in the heart of every flower,
   There glows the Beauty of His Power.

TO A FELLOW TRAVELLER ON LIFE'S ROAD

Friend, do you know that deep within your soul,
   There lies the wisdom that can make you whole?
And that within your heart there dwells a light
   That can transform to day life's darkest night?

Friend, do you know that God in heaven above,
   Guards you forever with eternal love?
That His Compassion, like a fragrant flower,
   Sweetens each moment of life's darkest hour?

When on life's path, you falter, stumble, fall,
   Wounded, afraid, and lonely, do you call
To One Who ever waits with outstretch'd hand
   To heal and comfort? When again you stand

Renewed in strength and power to take your place,
   Do you give thanks to God for His Sweet Grace?
And do you bravely share the pain of loss
   With Him Who gave His Son upon the Cross?

TO BABA ON HIS PASSING

Hast Thou withdrawn the Spirit from the Form?
But it was ever thus,
For what we saw and felt was but Illusion.
Always Thy stand was on a higher plane
Than we could comprehend.
The Son of God dwells not upon the earth,
But in his Father's House where Angels sing.
The Son of Man but shows His Form to us,
And then withdraws, that we may follow Him,
To those high realms of Beauty and Peace
Where all are One in perfect harmony,
And where His Presence and His Company
We may enjoy through eternity.

BABA

Thou art the quiet of the dawn
   Thou art the peacefulness of night.
Thou art the fragrance of a rose,
   Thou art the loveliness of light.

A meadow dreaming in the sun,
   The beauty of a crimson flower,
The snow that falls on winter fields,
   The sweetness of an April shower.

And yet the love of thee, dear Lord,
   Of quiet beauty hath no part,
It is a storm within my soul,
   It is a sword thrust thru my heart.

A cross of pain on which I hang,
   The cruel nails in hands and feet.
How cans't thou cause such agony,
   And yet bestow a love so sweet?

LOVE SONG
To Shri Meher Baba

I have no life save in the thought of Thee,
I have no joy save in the knowledge
  of Thy existence,
And no remembrance save of Thy Beauty.

Day and night I dwell in a world composed only of
  my love for Thee,
And in my ears is the music of Thy voice,
And the song of Thy laughter.

The stars are but reflections of the light
  of thine eyes,
And the warmth of the sun brings back
  the feel of Thine arms about me.

Others speak to me, but I hear only Thy words;
People pass me, and I see only Thee.
All my longing and desire and unsanctified
  passion are but for Thee alone,
For Thou art the fulfillment of my
  highest aspirations,
And the answer to all my prayers.

**AVATAR
MEHER BABA
KI JAI**

www.ingramcontent.com/pod-product-compliance
Lightning Source LLC
Chambersburg PA
CBHW021409290426
44108CB00010B/458